Kathleen Jelly Bean! Queen Lots of love

Acknowledgements

I have so many wonderful people to thank for this book.

My husband, my soul mate, my best friend in the world, the love of my life who loves me just as I am.

My mother, who taught me to color outside the lines. She was my first art teacher. When I was four, she asked me what would happen if I used the purple crayon to make polka dots on tree trunks in a coloring book. Life has never been the same since.

Prudence Mapstone, Margaret Hubert, and Jean Leinhauser, who mentored me throughout this whole process and beyond. I definitely couldn't have done it without you.

To Fiona Watts, whose gorgeous garden is my daily inspiration.

My fiber family, far and wide. Stitch Café in Valley Village, CA, and The International Freeform Crochet Guild and Crochet Guild of America who inspire me daily with creativity and friendships like no other.

To Melanie Gill, who encouraged me to speak with my authentic voice and let the world know about this utterly crazy passion.

And to my dear friend Vicki Woodyard just because.

In your light I learn how to love.

In your beauty, how to make poems.

You dance inside my chest,

where no one sees you,

but sometimes I do,

and that sight becomes this art.

-Jelaluddin Rumi 1207--1273

(Excerpts from *The Essential Rumi*, translations by Coleman Barks with John Moyne, 1995).

Rumi describes so perfectly the feeling I get from the creative flow, a visiting entity that I am blessed to have come stay within me for a while amid a chaotic world. I find that freeform, like no other art, sweeps me away into a space where I can dance with the timeless. I feel a sense of freedom as my fingers rejoice to their own beat.

The uninterrupted motion of creating loop after loop becomes so trancelike that I feel the rhythm of the universe and hear the hum of our glorious planet spinning along so that I can't help but connect with it, even for just a fleeting moment.

I know that my thoughts and to-do lists will reappear before long. The phone will ring or something will disturb the flow. But I also know that whenever I feel the stress of life, there is a space I can return to where I can dip my toes into that endless stream that's been available to all throughout human history. And through needlearts I find my home again. And for this I am grateful.

Publisher
Woodworks Editions
Sherman Oaks, CA

Book Editor
Ida Walker

Photographers
Page Wood
Myra Wood

Layout & Design
Steve Klippenstein
Myra Wood

Printer
Printed in China by Everbest Printing Co.
through Four Colour Imports, Ltd.,
Louisville, Kentucky.

Models
Arden Cho
Brookelyn Zeigler
Dawn Jeffory-Nelson
Gail Netherly-Grigsby
Haily Bond
Julia Marchese
Maya Washington
Megan Novak
Minky and Morty Wood
Sophia Haag

WW

A Woodworks Editions book
www.myrawood.com

Creative Crochet Lace:
A Freeform Look at Classic Crochet

ISBN-13: 978-0-9800182-9-5
ISBN-10: 0-9800182-9-3

First publication in 2008 by Woodworks Editions
Text and Photography © 2007 Myra Wood

Contents

Freeform Crochet Lace

Materials and Tools

The Five Styles

Some Finishing Touches

Laying the Foundation

If you already crochet, you most likely have had the pleasure of making garments, afghans, or other beautiful things using a pattern from a book or magazine. Freeform is one of the more creative aspects of crochet, a method of "fiber doodling." It's different from any other style of crochet. There are no planned instructions and no written patterns. You're free to explore the wonders of combining stitches and fibers to create whatever your heart desires. It's like a whole new world of discovery. Though you're using the same hook and fiber you've used before, you'll discover how to use them in a new and creative way.

If you already freeform, then you've already discovered for yourself how exhilarating the process can be. I'm going to show you how to do variations in crochet lace that will excite you even more!

Never having been one to color within the lines, I have an overwhelming infatuation for anything that's a little different from the norm so freeform was a natural for me when I stumbled on it. The process of creating Freeform Crochet Lace (which I'll refer to as FCL throughout the book) is one of discovery, ex-perimentation, and individual creativity. The more traditional method of repeating stitch patterns in rows or rounds are for other styles of crochet.

The instructions in this book are meant to be an inspiration and guide to various methods of thinking more creatively about your crochet. I want you to experience the same sense of wonder I've found from using this method. All of the usual crochet techniques are incorporated, and almost any stitch from traditional crochet and crochet lace making can be combined to achieve extraordinary results. Essentially, freeform crochet uses all the same skills as traditional crochet, but with a slightly different creative twist.

My approach is more of a fluid process than a set of specific A to Z steps, so I won't bother explaining all the crochet basics or specific stitches. I do encourage you to collect and study as many crochet stitch guides as you can to learn the multitude of possible stitches, motifs, and lace patterns that you can include in your work. Stitch guides can be your best friends! They offer you many variations that are really just combinations of the stitches

The doily on the left page is a freeform lace scrumble done in #10 cotton thread and a 1.5mm hook.

devastating effects of poverty. Selling handmade crochet could literally mean a family's survival. Many families had specific design motifs and protected them like family jewels. The finished works became heirlooms and were passed down through the generations; many still survive. I'm fortunate to have three delicate collars you saw on the previous pages made for my grandmother-in-law's birth in Northern Ireland in 1899. Irish Crochet and Clone's Lace are still done in Ireland and all over the world by its devoted followers.

By the turn of the century, crochet had spread throughout the industrialized world. It was no longer only a source of income. It was a beloved pastime that many women, men, and children enjoyed. Crochet skills spread throughout North America as people migrated west. After all, crochet was relatively quick to learn and very portable, perfect for the long trek.

Through the 20th century, crochet enjoyed periods of popularity, peaking midcentury with the advent of "modern crochet." Designers now took crochet to another level by creating wearable art.

As these modern crochet techniques emerged with a number of incredible fiber artists writing some spectacular books in the '70s, freeform crochet rose to worldwide visibility with the publication of what we freeformers commonly refer to as the freeform bible: *The Crochet Workbook*, written by James Walters and Sylvia Cosh in 1989. They introduced crotcheters to a new word and concept in crocheting: "scrumbling." Their approach combined crochet stitches in different directions to make small fragments of crocheted material they called "scrumbles."

The scrumbles were fit together like puzzle pieces and joined to make a larger freeform piece of crocheted fabric that typically fit into a template for a garment, accessory, or wall hanging.

Since the introduction of early scrumbling/freeform crochet in the United States and UK during the 1970s, many other crochet artists began to experiment with freeform crochet styles of their own. Most notable among these are Prudence Mapstone, Margaret Hubert, and Jenny Dowde, each who have written wonderful books listed in the reference section that I highly recommend.

What Is Freeform Crochet Lace?

Freeform crochet lace making is a fun and fulfilling adaptation of all the wonderful traditions of crochet rolled into one. The vast array of smooth and novelty yarns now available are combined with a variety of hook sizes. What makes it unique from traditional lace-making styles is that, like "regular" freeform (if you can say such a thing!) crochet, there aren't any patterns to follow. In essence, freeform doesn't really have any rules but you do need a basic understanding of crochet stitches, attention to the overall color of your piece and a sense of the general design. It sounds scary to have so much freedom and to wing it without a pattern, but it's actually a very relaxing and pleasurable process. FCL is fluid and relatively fast to do. You'll watch magic happen before your eyes! The best part is, even though it looks complicated, anyone who can make a simple single and double crochet stitch can learn to do it.

Artists of all kinds talk about finding their own unique style or voice. The whole freeform approach is one of freedom and abandonment. It's all about the journey and the endless discoveries possible. "Journey" is really a great word for describing this kind of art form since it's about the process. You will find your own spirit emerge as the pieces you create take on a life of their own. It's important not to lose sight of actually doing the work itself. It's easy to get caught up in wanting to see what it's going to be, but if you let go and follow your fingers, wonderful things can happen.

I think one of the best ways to practice this is the same way we learn any new creative process. Learn the basics first, and then improvise and riff away. Freeform is really a form of fiber jazz or contemporary dance with a hook and string. Watch the stitches as they leave the hook and melt into each other. Watch how one joins into the next to create new shapes. Get into the rhythm of the dance and zone out—but stay in the moment with your work and see where it goes. It will speak to you, and the whole notion of having preconceived ideas of what the finished product looks like will fall away.

You'll also discover design abilities you didn't even know you had. It's exciting for me to create a new piece every time I work on another creation. I still discover a new twist or turn on things I already

knew. You'll be creating whole new styles of your own in no time. I want you to take what you discover here and keep experimenting and adapting to find a style that suits you and should also be a style that you really love. It should never be uncomfortable or unpleasant. Some forms of crochet aren't as easy or as much fun as others for everyone. The best thing about freeform is that you will find a way that suits you, so you don't have to settle for something you don't love doing. You may even experiment with other freeform artists' styles for a while, which is a great way to start, but it won't take long to see your creations take on their own unique form. The most exciting thing about FCL is that no two pieces ever look alike; everything you make will become an original work of art.

I am obviously wild about all things freeform! By combining some traditional crochet lace techniques with freeform crochet methods I've learned over the past several years, I came up with five variations that will inspire you to take your traditional or freeform crochet to another level of creativity. It's important to understand that FCL is more of a mind-set than a specific plan

to follow. I'll often have an idea of what I want to create, something like a vest or a shawl, but I have no idea until it's done what it's going to look like. After I've finished, I sit and can't help but stare in amazement at where the journey led me.

The word "free," in all its connotations, is very important when talking about freeform crochet. There are as many different ways to create a freeform piece as the number of people doing it. Thousands of people worldwide consider crochet their fiber art of choice because it lends itself naturally to organic shapes more than most other methods. People often, mistakenly, think of crochet as just a method for making afghans and clothing, but full museum, fine-art installations, and sculptures have been created using traditional crochet techniques as well.

I learned to crochet as a child from my mother, but then left it for many years. Later, as an adult, I rediscovered it as a way to help balance my crazy work life. I found it very meditative, a much-needed sanctuary to unwind from a hectic day. I loved the act of hooking yarn, but I was bored to tears following pattern instructions. Besides,

I wasn't crazy about making yet another granny square afghan! (No disrespect intended! I made my share and still love them.) Typically I'd abandon the pattern after a few rows and improvise anyway. I've always adored the look of crochet openwork, and I made lots of lacy crochet wearables and doily patterns, but something was always "missing." I was a graphic artist, but it had never occurred to me to use crochet in such an incredibly creative way!

I first stumbled on Walters and Cosh's The Crochet Workbook in 1990 and fell in love immediately. My work life was too busy, but it always stuck in my mind to try methods explained in the Workbook. A few years later, I stumbled onto freeform crochet through an accidental search on the internet. I discovered a world of wonderful artists all doing the amazing form of crochet I'd seen earlier. Prudence Mapstone, Margaret Hubert, and Bonnie Pierce became my guides to, literally, uncharted territories. My heart soared when I realized the possibilities available through freeform. I located the Walters/Cosh book on my shelf and started experimenting. It was all starting to make sense, but it

wasn't until a year later, when I was lucky enough to take Prudence's workshop, that a whole new world was opened to me! I remember taking her incredible two-day class and not sleeping for days afterward because a newly discovered fountain of inspiration was welling up from my creative depths. I was like a fiber demon unleashed, and my stash grew and grew as I tried more and more yarns I'd never tried before and never even knew existed. The variety of fibers available now is inspiration enough! The whole time I was learning this wonderful technique using heavier yarns, I couldn't help but think about what it would be like to make crochet lace in a freeform style with thread and finer-weight cotton yarns. I loved making those traditional crochet lace styles so much that I started to experiment with various lace stitches I knew. I came up with methods of scrumbling with lace crochet. Since then, I've developed five forms of freeform crochet lace, all loosely based on traditional styles. I call them Funky Filet, Tossed Salad Style, Wild Irish Crochet, Doodle Lace, and Organic Lace Scrumbling. In each variation, the work grows organically as you

stitch, and you will see results immediately. You have infinite opportunities to change and alter the design at any time.

I'll introduce you to each style in just a bit, and then we'll wind our way around with a variety of stitches to create a unique, magical, one-of-a-kind fabric of your own special creation. Each of my styles has a different approach, but the one thing they all have in common is they're done without any written instructions. Instead of row-by-row directions, I'll give you the tools you need to create your own unique creative lace by explaining basic concepts and examples so you have the freedom to invent as you go.

I prefer flat lace work with surface embellishments that is fairly open and airy, but you may prefer to make a more piled or sculptural fabric, or possibly something thinner and wispier like a gossamer web. Some of these techniques may be more enjoyable than others, and you might prefer how certain ones look. It never hurts to try something at least once just to find out whether you like it.

The best part of freeform is that there really are no mistakes. Get excited about the possibilities and be inspired by your own endless imagination. Throw caution to the wind! Go crazy! Scrumble your heart out - let your threads and yarns speak to you! Follow your fingers and see where they lead you. I'm sure you'll find the same joy and inspiration from FCL that I do.

Freeform Lace as Art and Self-Discovery

Before we delve into the particulars of the techniques, I think it's vital to absorb an essential aspect of FCL I mentioned briefly before. Doing freeform is an incredibly inspiring process, but it's easy to think in terms of making specific things and find you become too caught up in wanting the finished piece. I enjoy the craft of crocheting, and I love that I know how to create something useful. Freeform allows me to experience the wonder of fiber art at the same time that I'm doing a craft. I wander from stitch to stitch and watch as it all unfolds. This is part of the age-old discussion of process versus product. Freeform allows me to sit with something and see where it takes me . . . rather than know where the journey will end before I get there. There is an art to that, itself, which I only experience when I'm fully immersed in what I'm doing.

We spend so much time rushing from one thing to the next, with the endless to-do list replaying in our heads all day long, that sometimes we forget to just sit. As soon as I sit with hook in hand, I fall into a place of peace to just be, and the creativity flows. I lose track of time completely. When I am finally finished, I'm always amazed that every thread holding the whole thing together was deliberately set by my own hand. I'm still tickled by the fact that the final cloth is really just one long, intertwining thread.

One of the main obstacles for many crotcheters just beginning to do FCL is being too critical of their work. It's very natural to be hard on yourself or to feel intimidated or overwhelmed. A lot of people stop themselves before they even get started, thinking they aren't creative or they aren't "artists." Everyone has the ability to unleash his or her own creative side. While you are crocheting, take it one stitch at a time and reserve any judgment about what you are doing. The first steps are only the beginning, and each piece grows into a splendidly woven fabric the more you work on it. You'll find if you're not particularly happy with one area, it transforms into something else you may love as you continue to work.

Lose yourself in your crochet. Since this is freeform, just allow yourself to watch what you are doing instead of making any decisions about its worthiness. Pick a theme or find a photo that inspires you, and let your fingers wander without trying to make something specific happen. Freeform is really a form of impressionism and expressionism, so feel the piece during the process. Pick a yarn you absolutely adore, use your favorite hook, and explore the possibilities as you feel the fiber flow through your fingers stitch by stitch. You'll be very surprised with just how easy and freeing freeforming really is! Surrendering all preconceived notions and worries about what something is "supposed to be" is actually very liberating. Many times I start out with one idea in mind only to end up in a whole different place, one that I could never have dreamed of had I tried designing it beforehand.

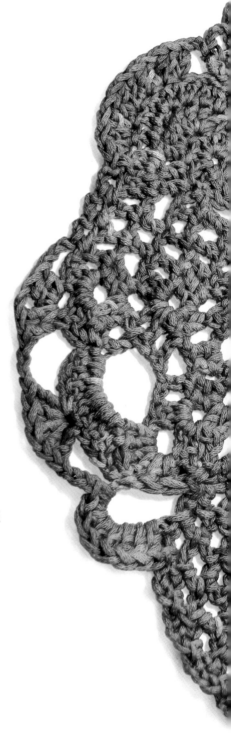

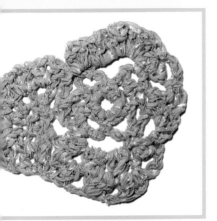

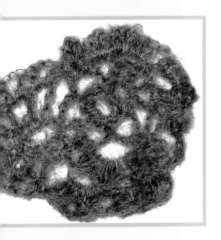

The same 3 scrumbles made with the same size hook but different yarns.

Materials and Tools
Yarn and Thread

The process of crocheting lace is actually much easier than it looks and requires only a few simple tools. One of the most exciting things to happen in the fiber world in many years has been the introduction of a huge amount of gorgeous natural and synthetic fibers. You can get them in local yarn shops or even online. The mind-boggling array of colors, textures, blends, and exotic threads can be incorporated into differnt styles of FCL. Even the less expensive, more commercial brands now include a huge assortment of unique novelty yarns and natural fibers.

Yarn shopping has never been more fun (and addictive!) Your personal collection of yarn is commonly referred to as your stash, and many people, including myself, suffer from a syndrome known as SABLE (Stash Acquired Beyond Lifetime Expectancy). Many of the newest and silkiest fibers can be used with more traditional cotton threads and yarns in freeform crochet lace making. Remember, since this is freeform, you can use as many different fibers as you can find. Experiment and see the different effects and what you most like using. The same stitches done in different fibers can have a totally different feeling and drape.

Natural yarns are now available in fibers made from such widely diverse materials as soy, bamboo, banana, recycled sari silk, flax, and hemp, to name just a few. The colors are gorgeous, and the yarns come in many weights and textures. For a lighter, lacier fabric, I like finer fingering, DK, and sport weight, smooth yarns to show off your lace. The more texture a yarn has, the less are able to see the delineation of each stitch. Still, there's no reason why you can't explore bulkier or fluffier mohair yarns too for a fuzzier effect. I tend to use more natural fibers when I want a more organic feel to my finished piece.

There are also a multitude of synthetic and novelty yarns that include metallic fibers and fluffy bits that are also delicious for lace designs. Many of these yarns are great for a glitzier or more formal look. Just a hint of them mixed in or as an embellishment will add a spark to an otherwise plain piece. I like to use those yarns in Tossed Salad pieces and in the surface embellishments I add to a piece when it's finished.

My favorite yarns are 100% cotton yarns and threads, especially hand-dyed fibers that

Crochet Hooks

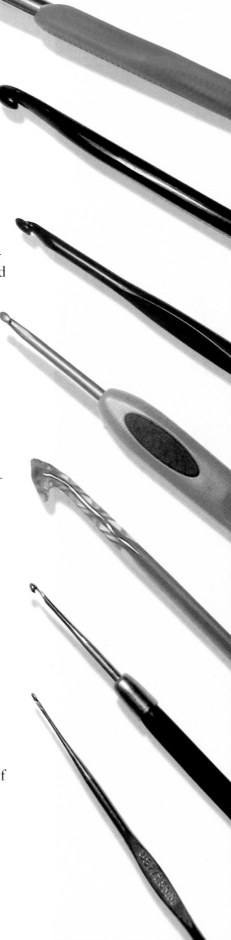

are available through specialty yarn stores or online sellers. Perle and pima cottons have such gorgeous textures and smooth sheens that they lend themselves to making beautiful lace items. Experiment with them, and see which fibers speak most loudly and clearly to you. Traditional lace threads, often called bedspread or crochet thread, now come in a whole spectrum of colors. The higher the number on the thread package, the thinner the thread. Threads commonly used for crochet lace can be as fine as size 100 or 150, but I usually use something that's at least a size 10 or 3.

There are tons of inexpensive "kitchen" cotton yarns, considered worsted weight and typically used to make dishcloths. They are inexpensive to practice with and have a look of their own that works for more informal items. I like using them for shopping bags or totes and household items like pillows, which I know will get more wear. As is the case with any fiber art you do, the better quality yarns will always give you a richer looking piece and are most always worth the investment, considering all the time and effort you are taking to make something by hand.

Absolutely any style of crochet hook can be used for freeform lace, and there's a whole world of hooks available, from the basic mass-produced ones to the finely handcrafted collectible versions. Each hook brings with it unique opportunities to create something new and wonderful. To start, try every style you can get your hands on, from a thin steel hook to a slightly larger steel hook, to the larger aluminum or bamboo or bone hooks (usually sized by letters), to the specially hand-turned woods or hand-forged metal hooks. A standard hook, best suited for most yarns, can be made of practically any material: plastic, wood, and aluminum—even glass. I love collecting hooks and have quite a few handmade ones that give me great joy to use.

Try different sizes to see what you're most comfortable using. Typically, fine crochet lace is done with crochet cotton thread and a steel hook, but since we are freeforming, exact size isn't restricted regardless of which type of hook you use. I know that when I use a DK weight yarn, I like to use an F/ 3.75 mm hook for a lacy effect. If I want the overall fabric to have a tighter weave, I'll move down

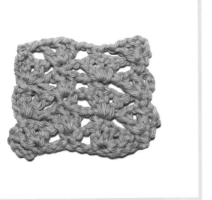

Three pieces of lace made with the same stitches and yarn but with increasingly larger hooks.

to a D/2.75mm or E/3.5mm, and if I'm using a worsted-weight yarn or want an even lacier look, I'll go up to a G/4mm or H/5mm. You can achieve a lacier fabric just by using a hook a couple sizes larger than you'd ordinarily use for a certain yarn. I personally like to stay with the smaller hooks because they give me the look I like most, but I encourage you to try different sizes with different yarns to see how a simple change of hook size can change the look of the stitches.

My favorites are aluminum hooks set into plastic handles, but you'll find the ones that work best for you. At this point I probably need to warn you about crochet hook addiction, since there are so many incredible handmade hooks available.

Because lace work is finer than work using heavier yarns and larger hooks, make sure to take breaks and stretch your hands. When I'm using steel hooks, I'll often keep going, and before I realize it my hands are cramping up. Hold your hook with a firm grip, but not too tightly, and stretch your fingers at least once an hour. I like to do a simple hand exercise when I use steel hooks. I clench my

fist tightly for a few seconds and then open my hands and stretch my fingers as wide as possible. I repeat that about five times and go back to crocheting. It's amazing how much better your hands will feel if you just do this one exercise regularly.

You can also wrap your hooks to make them thicker if you find that using a steel hook is too uncomfortable. Surgical tape wrapped around and around the handle/shank of the hook works well. I've even used hair scrunchies to pad the handles. If you get really industrious, you can build a polymer clay handle to make your very own customized steel hook (make sure to follow the polymer clay manufacturer's instructions). Deborah Doyle, a woodcrafter who sinks the hooks into gorgeous rosewood-turned handles makes my favorite steel hooks in the world. They feel absolutely luscious.

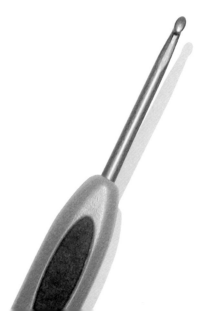

Templates

Templates are as important as the yarn and hook when you're doing FCL. Used like tailoring or dressmaking patterns or quilting templates, they provide the foundation that gives you the freedom to let go and be creative using a general plan for sizing. Even if you're doing a continuous piece of Funky Filet, Doodle Lace, or Tossed Salad that's created in one continuous piece, you still need a template for a reference and to check sizing as you work.

In a perfect world it's great to leave a template flat throughout an entire project. But due to space restrictions (like actually needing to eat at your dining room table), you may need to fold up your project while you're not working on it. I like to use a large piece of corrugated cardboard and tape my template to it. All of your crocheted pieces eventually fill in the whole template, so it's convenient to be able to leave it on a flat surface till it's finished, with the added benefit that the cardboard is easily moveable while your work is in process. You can cut desired shapes for the template from a large roll of construction or drawing paper or a plain piece of cotton muslin. You can also use Polarfleece or interfacing fabrics as the template material as well. For large garments or throws it's easier to work with a fabric template as it's handy to pin the crochet pieces to it, and fabric folds up easily when you're not working on your project. Since a template gets quite a bit of use throughout the project, it's best to stay away from thinner, traditional tissue-paper pattern papers used in standard home sewing/tailoring patterns. Like traditional sewing patterns, however, FCL templates—when properly made—can be reused many times.

I like to create a template for everything I make (even if it's something as simple as a square pillow) so I have an overall design guide and something to fit my piece or pieces to as I make them. If I want to make a simple square or rectangular item like a handbag I cut a piece of cardboard to the exact size I want. Then I have a visual reference at all times to see how much more I need to stitch or add in any direction.

It's very easy to create a template from an existing garment or object. If it's something you will wear, the fit is crucial. I like to use an item that fits me well as my guide. You can use a commercial clothing pattern,

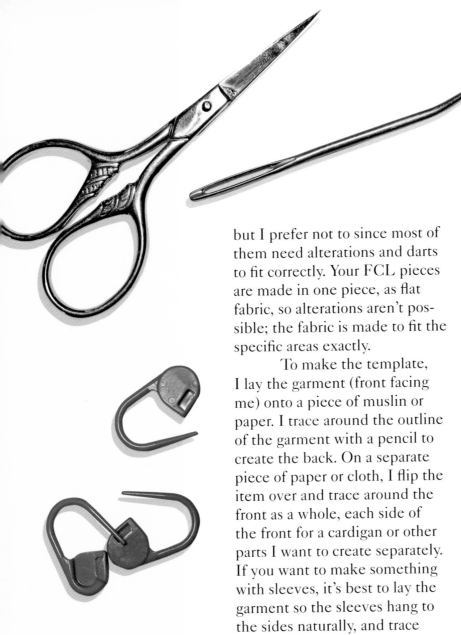

but I prefer not to since most of them need alterations and darts to fit correctly. Your FCL pieces are made in one piece, as flat fabric, so alterations aren't possible; the fabric is made to fit the specific areas exactly.

To make the template, I lay the garment (front facing me) onto a piece of muslin or paper. I trace around the outline of the garment with a pencil to create the back. On a separate piece of paper or cloth, I flip the item over and trace around the front as a whole, each side of the front for a cardigan or other parts I want to create separately. If you want to make something with sleeves, it's best to lay the garment so the sleeves hang to the sides naturally, and trace around the entire item as one piece. Once the tracing is done, fold the paper or muslin in half to make sure it will be symmetrical and adjust as necessary. If the item you want to make is a cardigan style, create a separate template for each side of the front by tracing around one half of the garment only and cut two pieces the exact same size or use the one piece for both sides and flip it over so they match.

There are a number of ways to fill in the template depending on which method you

use to create your piece. We'll talk about the different styles in a second. The general idea is that you're making a fabric that fits the entire surface of the template. Taking the time to create a template before beginning to crochet your project will let you relax and crochet without worrying about how something will fit later.

Work Surfaces and Lighting

One of the most important tools you need for making FCL is a firm, flat surface. I like to use large pieces of flat cardboard that transfer easily to a desk, table, or onto my lap. Once your template is created, secure it to a piece of cardboard, just slightly larger than the template with masking or package tape. That way it's easy to move the whole project without disturbing your work. You can even stow it under a bed if you won't be working on it for some time. Storage, moving and shipping companies have large pieces you can buy for the size you need. It's also very important that your work stay flat as you create your fabric so having a good sturdy base will allow you to check it constantly to make sure it's behaving. You can easily check your work against a flat surface to make sure it's not pulling too tightly or bunching up from too many stitches in one area. I'll go into this in more detail on pages 24 and 25.

Lighting is also essential. It's definitely worth it to invest in a good lamp. A proper light source will protect your eyes and make it easier to do your crochet. After all, it's always nice to be able to see what you're doing! I love the daylight/ full spectrum bulbs that are available from office supply stores and many sewing and craft stores. They're great for working at night and fit into most desk lamps. The color of the light is more natural than incandescent bulbs, so colors are more authentic.

Other Useful Tools

There are a few other things you'll need, and they are readily available at most yarn, fabric, or craft stores. You'll need a good pair of small scissors (3½ inch embroidery scissors or little sheathed snippets) for cutting

yarn and thread tails, a tapestry needle (maybe two sizes) for sewing seams, and lots of safety pins to hold your pieces together as you work on your project. My most favorite "pins" are actually small plastic stitch markers, used in knitting, that open like a regular safety pin but there are no sharp corners to snag your fibers. You will find it much easier to work and to transport your work if you start with a large two-gallon clear plastic zipper bag to store your work in progress (WIP) until it's finished. When a WIP bag is neglected or forgotten, the contents are later, very commonly referred to as unfinished objects (UFOs). We all have at least one of those! But hopefully, you'll be so inspired to finish that you won't have any and you'll be the proud creator of many FOs (finished objects). Once you start acquiring a good stash of yarns and threads, invest in clear plastic containers with lids to sort and see all your stuff. I like to sort my yarns by color so having them in individual containers I can see through makes it a snap to find what I need.

One optional item I can't praise enough is a dress form, which is available in fabric stores and used to fit and alter sewn

21

Adjustable dress form

clothing. I don't know what I'd ever do without mine! Although you'll have a template created to the exact size of the piece you are making, a dress form in your size will ensure a perfect fit. It's great to work back and forth between the template and the dress form to alter the fit of whatever you make while it's being created.

The trick is to find a dress form that's just a tiny bit bigger than you are. Once the item is done, it's guaranteed to fit perfectly. Many forms are adjustable so give yourself an extra inch for each measurement so that the garment isn't too tight. While I work I often move the connected pieces from the template to the dress form and back again to check how they fit and hang. I've even used the dress form itself as my template, pinning the scrumbles right onto it and sewing them together directly on the form. You can easily create a very fitted garment this way! I usually start at the shoulders and work my way down, adding on pieces as I go. This way I can also move scrumbles around to fit the dress form perfectly before sewing them together.

Where Do I Start?
Lace Logic

Before you experiment with creating your own complex lace patterns, I suggest starting by finding a lace stitch you love in a stitch guide and working a few sets of the lace pattern to get a feel for how lace patterns work. Once you're comfortable with openwork stitches, you can set up your own lace patterns using "lace logic." Any stitch can be combined with chains to create an open pattern. When you want to create a space in your fabric, you do chain stitches to open that area. For example, if you did two double crochets next to each other, you would create a dense fabric. But, if you did the same two double crochets with one or more chain stitches between them, you create a lacier look. When you combine the chains and stitches over several rows, you'll start to see a looser, more open fabric develop. The more chains you use between stitches, the larger your holes will be and the lighter the final fabric will be too. When making large garments, it may be more appropriate to create a lighter fabric.

If you are making something smaller, something in which fabric weight isn't an issue, you might go with fewer chains between stitches and create a tighter fabric. Decide before starting your project how tight or loose you want the fabric to be and then keep it consistent as you go. You can easily do a little swatch of stitches with different hooks and the same yarn to see the result. Of course there are times when you may want to combine larger and smaller areas of stitches that may require different hook sizes to achieve the desired effect. It's totally up to you (and there is no wrong way), although we will go into design and balance later for deciding what's most appropriate. The size of the hook you pick and the weight of the yarn or thread will have a lot to do with the density of your fabric as well.

When you move to a new row, you have the choice to crochet into an already created space or to continue chaining to make an even larger space. One popular method is to make a chain loop on one row and fill it with double crochets on the next. This creates a fan of crochet stitches, with an open pattern holding it together. One way to achieve this is to chain 5, let's say, between two stitches and then doing double crochets spaced with 2 or more chains on the next row.

Five Styles of Freeform Crochet Lace

Let's explore five different styles of freeform crochet lace so that you get the hang of each and see what makes them unique. Each of these styles borrows loosely from more traditional styles. I'll explain the technique I use, but I also encourage you to combine any of them and come up with your own. By learning these techniques and using them along with other crochet methods, your individual style will emerge naturally in no time. The best part about freeform is that no two pieces are ever alike; they are unique from the beginning.

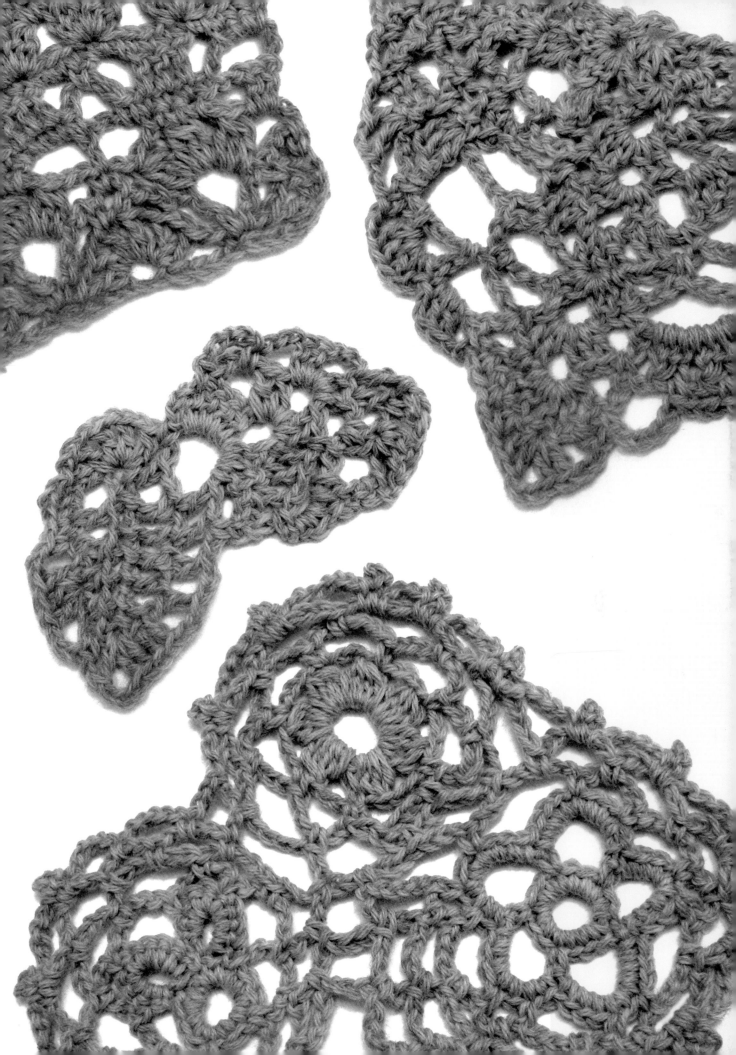

Funky Filet

The easiest way to jump into FCL is Funky Filet, which is based on a traditional style called "filet crochet." The name comes from the French: the verb "filer" meaning to spin or to draw out, and the French noun "filet" meaning "thread" or "net." Filet crochet is usually worked from a pattern and diagram to create a picture or decorative design over a series of squares in a grid format (thus, the "net") from one row to the next. There are specific, limited stitches used, which we'll learn shortly, but instead of following a set pattern, all of the basic filet stitches are repeated randomly to create a completely abstract pattern over the final fabric. Ordinarily, one thread or yarn is used throughout the whole project to unify the entire piece.

In traditional filet, a series of blocks are made, row-by-row. Each block is a multiple of double crochets and/or chains over a series of the same number of stitches. It's usually broken down into 4 or 5 stitch patterns over the whole row which can be combinations of double crochets or chains totaling that amount as indicated by a chart or pattern. For Funky Filet, the filet is done in a similar way, starting at one end of a row and finishing at

the other, but there's no pattern or preset design.

Exercise

Let's do a 5-block filet pattern to start. Each block consists of a double crochet at the beginning and end for the sides of the block and variations on the 3 chains or stitches in between.

Grab a G hook and DK or worsted weight yarn and chain 25. To start the first block, chain 3 more which will count as your first double crochet. Double crochet into the 5th chain from the hook to make the second double crochet in the block. Double crochet into the next 3 chains. You now have 5 double crochets, which make up the first block. The next block uses the last double crochet made as its first side. You have the choice of doing several different things over the next three chains. Remember that you need to end with 1 double crochet as the 5th stitch for the other side of the next block and each block after it. You can chain three or skip the next three chains and double crochet into the fourth chain to make an empty block. To fill a block you would do 4 double crochets over the next 4 chains. You can also skip any of the chains by chaining one and doing a double crochet into the next stitch between the two sides of the block.

Just remember that each block will be 5 stitches wide, including the first and last double crochet, and each last double crochet of 5 becomes the first double crochet of the next block and counts as the last of one and the first of the next. To continue to the next row, chain 3 and turn. This turning chain counts as your first double crochet in the first block of the next row. Now repeat the process of making blocks over the next row. When you get to the end of the row, double crochet into the 3rd chain of the turning chain. Chain 3, turn, and continue as you desire.

Another stitch used frequently in filet crochet is the lacet. The lacet looks like a V stitch in the middle of a block. To do a lacet, at the beginning of a block, chain 2, skip a stitch, and single crochet into the second chain or double crochet below, chain 2, and finish the block with a double crochet into the 5th double crochet or chain of the block on the previous row.

Try a few rows of as many stitch variations as you can make, randomly placed, so that

Garden Goddess
Funky Filet Top

you can see the effect. After four or five rows, you will see abstract patterns emerge from the randomly placed solid blocks within the openwork mesh. Funky filet works up very quickly, so you can easily make a wearable garment in just a few evenings.

Increases are done by adding multiples at the end of a row. When you turn, add 3 chains for the first double crochet, and work across the new chains as if they were stitches from the previous row, making sure to keep an even count for each block. It's very easy to create sleeves using this method. For decreases at the beginning of a row, just slip stitch across the stitches you want to decrease, and start your blocks accordingly. If you decrease to the middle of a block from the previous row, consider the next stitch or chain as the same number on a grid as the space below it. Don't start a new block from that point. Continue across, lining up the blocks with the previous row.

To decrease at the end of a row, just leave the desired number of stitches unworked, chain 3, and turn to start the next row. Again, it's really important to make sure your blocks line up correctly, so check the block below to see where you are starting from and proceed accordingly.

This top was created by matching the shape to an existing crocheted top I made before that I knew fit well. I made it in 2 parts, front and back and joined the seams. Using a I hook and a chunky sari silk & wool blend yarn, I chained the width of the bottom of the original top and worked filet randomly from bottom to top. I increased on each side when I got to the arms to the width of the original sleeves and continued Funky Filet to the top edge. I created a back piece that was the identical size to the front piece I made. The neck shaping you see is just from blocking it into the correct shape before sewing the seams with a mattress stitch on each side, under the arms and the shoulders using the same yarn. Once I decided which would be the front and which would be the back by trying it on, I added a surface crochet ruffle as an embellishment, which you can read more about on page 55. Funky Filet makes a great base for adding flowers, embellishments or other scrumbly pieces.

Template made from an existing top

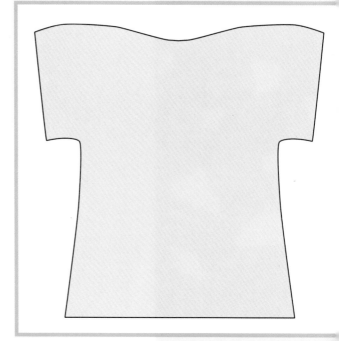

Doodle Lace

Doodle Lace is a fun technique, too. You're essentially doodling with a hook and fiber. With this technique, you start in the center, doing basic crochet stitches randomly in a flat circular method, allowing the piece to grow until it is as large as you'd like. You can also work from one side to another and turn your work each row if you want to make a half circle. There is no wrong way to make Doodle Lace, but I suggest using one yarn or thread throughout to unify your piece. The overall effect of doodling is busy, so using a common thread throughout will tie everything together and allow the eye to travel smoothly from one area to another.

Exercise

Start with a G or H hook and a DK or worsted-weight smooth yarn. Crochet a circle of 12 double crochets: chain 5, slip stitch to create a ring, and double crochet into the center, filling up the full circle. Making sure the circle lays flat before slip stitching to the first stitch to complete the circle. Chain 7, skip 2 double crochets, and single crochet into next stitch. Continue chaining in varying amounts and attaching to previous stitches around the circle, skipping a stitch or two as you go to create open loops. Do whatever combination of stitches you'd like in each loop, working around to the beginning of that row. Either slip stitch and chain to start the next row or just continue doing stitches into the tops of previous stitches. You may decide to do three double crochets in one loop, chain in between to the next loop, and 5 single crochets in the next loop. Make sure to add chains between loops and stitches to maintain a lacy look. At any point you can turn and work back around the other way.

You can stop in any area and flip back and forth, sort of short-rowing several times before moving to the next spot to keep the piece from becoming too symetrical.

Essentially, you are creating one large scrumble without breaking your yarn. You may choose to start another piece of Doodle Lace and join them, but the most important thing, as with all FCL . . . Keep it flat! As the piece grows, you may need to add more stitches or chains between the last stitches to keep it flat. I find it VERY helpful to work on a flat surface to ensure the fabric doesn't bunch or pull.

This started as one granny square circular motif and grew from there. Initially I worked in the round but then worked from side to side after a few rows to create a flat upper edge for the top of a shawl.

Create opportunities for larger open spaces by intentionally chaining a number of stitches to go back into on the following rounds with various crochet stitches.

Here you can see a large open space created by chaining 8 or 9 which works as the foundation hole for double crochet shells in the next rows.

Peacock Path
Doodle Lace Cape

This cape was created completely in Doodle Lace without breaking the yarn at any time. I used a hand-dyed 100% mohair yarn with a K hook to achieve the soft, fluffy fabric. It began on a lap desk and outgrew it quickly. I worked randomly from one side to the other, turning my work at the end of each row and working back. As you can see it eventually took over the sofa!

Jubilee
Tossed Salad Diagonal Top

The object of this design was to use a number of different yarns I love all in one piece. I used sari silk, chenille, hand-dyed cottons and even banana silk along with some novelty yarns. I simply made two rectangles the same size for the front and the back and then seamed them at the shoulders and sides. Each rectangle used different, random lace stitch patterns I made up as I went along using lace logic. It started with one stitch and increased one stitch at the beginning and the end of every other row to create and increase that made it a triangle. When I got to the point where it was wide enough to span my hips from side to side, I started decreasing one stitch at the beginning and end of every other row until I got back to 1 stitch. This created the other triangle and becomes an even rectangle. If you want to try this, any increase or decrease you want to do at the beginning or end of the rows will work so use one you're familiar with. I improvised the lace stitches over the rows as I went, determining which stitch pattern to use by the number of stitches I had to cross to complete the row. There's lots of room to fudge with FCL.

Because of the diagonal nature of this project, when the pieces were complete there was a natural amount of pulling to one side that I corrected by blocking both rectangles before seaming with a mattress stitch. I soaked each rectangle in warm water until they were saturated and pinned them to a piece of foam core with push-pins and let it dry in the sun over two days.

I decided to leave the neck, bottom edge and armholes unfinished rather than using a single crochet around so that lines of each row would flow more organically without framing the overall design.

Most of the yarns I used are normally too heavy to use for a solidly crocheted fabric but by using them with lace stitches I was able to make a garment that was much lighter and more comfortable to wear. Tossed Salad Lace is great for combining yarns you might not ordinarily think of using for crochet lace.

Wild Irish Crochet

I adapted Wild Irish Crochet from the popular method of crochet lace making developed in Europe in the mid-1800s called "Irish crochet," the original freeform! The traditional form is still done using specific floral or decorative motifs that are pinned or basted to a preset outline drawn on a piece of muslin fabric or paper. The motifs are then connected with variations of fill-in chain stitches, called filling stitches, to create a mesh background that holds the whole piece together.

With Wild Irish Crochet, various motifs are made first, placed randomly, and joined with a series of chains to create the mesh, just as in the traditional Irish Crochet. The differences between the techniques come in the choice of yarns, the size of the hook, and the motifs you choose. Traditional techniques ordinarily use a steel hook and fine thread.

You can do the very same techniques with Wild Irish Crochet using a big crochet hook and any yarn you want! Wild Irish Crochet uses some of the same Irish crochet motifs, but you can also create other fun motifs such as those based on granny squares and more modern designs. Wild Irish crochet can be done with a single color or with various colors for each motif and one color for the joining mesh; the joining color acts to pull the design together.

Exercise

Let's use a G hook and a smooth DK or sport-weight yarn. I like cotton since it borrows from the traditional style, but any smooth yarn will work. The novelty or fluffier yarns like mohair won't show your stitches as much so I like the plainer yarns for Wild Irish Crochet.

Create five random motifs of your choice using your stitch guides, granny square patterns or simply your imagination. You can easily start with chaining five, slip stitching to create a ring, and then single or double crocheting into the center to make a circle. Flat flower motifs and the center of granny squares are perfect for this style. Lay all five randomly on a table or board with about 2 inches between them. Start with any of the motifs and join your yarn to an edge of one of the motifs.

You'll be creating a simple mesh filling to join the motifs and make the fabric. Chain 5, skip 2 stitches, and single crochet into next stitch; repeat these chain loops all the

way around. Slip stitch to the first chain loop. Chain 5 and repeat this process around again, single crocheting into each previous chain loop. You may need to add more chains or do more loops to keep your fabric flat. You can also do more than one single crochet in each chain loop as you make a new loop. As you fill in the mesh between motifs and you come close to another motif join the next chain 5 with a slip stitch to the new motif. Work back and forth between the two motifs or around the new motif, chaining and joining to fill in between.

Once you reach a logical edge of the next motif, work around it in the same fashion. Work back and forth around the motifs, joining as you go and filling in any areas you can with the chain five loops. If you have areas that remain open and it's not possible to work back into them, leave them for the end. Join your yarn at the edge you want to fill in and chain across to fill in that area. Not all the filling stitches need to be done at the same time, but it's great if you can cover as much area as possible as you crochet. Continue to crochet the mesh around the motifs until you have all of them connected.

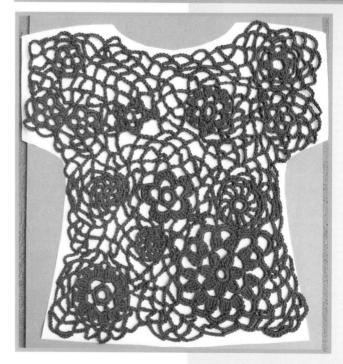

Morning Glory
Wild Irish Crochet Tunic

I started this top by tracing around another top I made in an openwork crochet pattern that I knew fit quite well. I used a piece of white construction paper from a long roll. Both sides of the top are identical so I used the same template for both. You can see pictures of the progress of this actual piece on page 41.

Once the template was taped to a large piece of cardboard so that it wouldn't move throughout the project, I started making random motifs from various granny square patterns and flower designs I improvised, making sure to vary the sizes for more interest in the overall design. I placed them randomly on the template and temporarily taped them into position. Starting with a motif in the lower left corner, I created the mesh fill-in stitches to cover the template as needed.

I let the shape of the template dictate how many stitches I needed and what shape to make them.

After completing the mesh to fit the template I made another side, with different motifs placed in different areas and filled that side in with mesh as well and pinned the two sides together using plastic stitch markers that look like safety pins. To create the seam and mimic the mesh stitches, I place the two sides next to each other with a gap of one inch and sewed a seam that mimicked the open mesh pattern with long stitches.

You can also crochet mesh seams between the two sides if you prefer by leaving a one inch space between the front and back, chaining from side to side and joining as you go. I decided to let the natural edge of the mesh become the hem and sleeve edges but you could do a traditional picot edging or anything else you like if you want a more finished or straighter edge.

A basic T-shirt shape works great modified as a template.

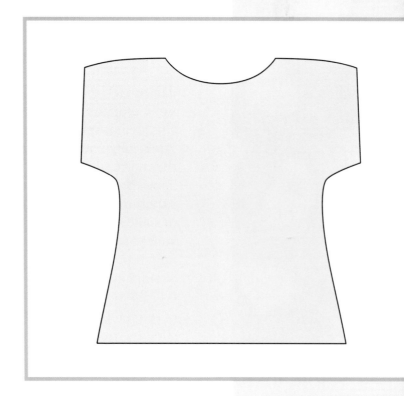

Organic Lace Scrumbling

Organic Lace Scrumbling is adapted from methods commonly used in more well known types of freeform crochet. This type of scrumbling is also done without any patterns to create expanses of flat fabric that typically fit into a template by creating separate pieces, each about the size of your palm and joining them like puzzle pieces to make the larger fabric. Instead of making a dense fabric with multiple yarns and yarn weights, as is typically done in more traditional scrumbling, Organic Lace Scrumbling is usually done with one yarn or one type of yarn throughout the whole piece. Any crochet or crochet lace stitches can be incorporated throughout to allow the design to flow freely, openly, and not too chaotically. Sometimes I like to pick three or four of the same type, weight, and brand of a particular yarn in shades of the same color and blend between them. I tend to use the same hook throughout, but you can experiment with changing sizes to achieve a different look to your stitches. Again, gauge isn't important since you're filling in a template. Since this method typically uses one type of yarn or thread throughout, the more stitches you learn and incorpo-

rate, the more interesting your work will be when it's finished. All crochet stitches are fair game when it comes to Organic Lace Scrumbling.

Exercise
Start with a G hook and DK weight yarn. Create a motif of your choice. I like to start with small, flat circles of 12 or so double crochets in a ring. As you go to the next row, start to work off the circle in all different directions. You can do different stitches around the center, then work halfway back across the next row, and then go off in a completely different direction. Since we are doing this lace style, you want to chain a few before, after, or between your stitches. I often do double crochets with a chain 1 between. Try popcorn stitches or shells with chains between as well. Be sure to work some chain loops onto the edge as you work around to set up for a shell stitch when you come back around. Once you have a palm-sized piece, break your yarn. Create other scrumbles with totally different stitches as in the top picture to the right.

After several scrumbles are made, you'll need to attach them in a style that mimics lace as closely as possible. When creating a dense fabric of freeform, it's usually done by taking the scrumbles and fitting them closely next to each other and tightly sewing or crocheting them together. With FCL, the joins would be too obvious that way, so the best method is to use lace stitches or a couple, minimal sewn stitches only at the points where one touches another . To sew the edge of one scrumble to another, pick just two or three points where one edge would touch another, like the middle picture to your right, and use a tapestry needle and the same yarn to sew only those points. Only use a couple of stitches to join so it looks like a continuation of the lace. That way it will retain the feeling of lace, rather than look like a flat seam. At this point you can continue to add stitches around the edges to fill in gaps or grow the piece larger, like the lower picture to the right, until the pice is a sufficient size to fit an area of the template. Keep your eye on your template so that the piece grows accordingly and doesn't overflow the edge.

Since you are using a template, it's very easy to place pieces where you want them, join them, and then continue to

scrumble around them, adding more stitches as you go.

When you are creating a larger garment or object there are two methods of scrumbling you can use. Experiment with both to see which you prefer: The first method is to fill the template full of scrumbles first, leaving an inch or so between each, pin or tape the pieces to the template to hold them in place and then make the fill-in stitches or sew the scrumbles together. The fill-in stitches are worked just as they are in Wild Irish crochet but you can use any stitches you want to join and crisscross from one scrumble to another.

The second way is to join two or three scrumbles and then fill in and add stitches of your choice around the piece in all different directions to create a larger section of fabric. Put that piece into your template and continue to make more scrumbles, attaching them to the larger piece and working into that larger piece as you go. There is less sewing with this method and more opportunity to crochet around and off of larger pieces. You can also do this by creating several large sections and then joining them with lace stitches. It's really your choice and you can decide what works

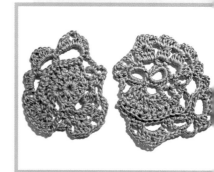

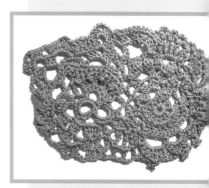

Evolution of a lace scrumble

best for you. Crocheting into larger pieces has more of a tendency to pucker and pull so as with all FCL . . . keep it flat!! For Organic Scrumbling, I prefer to build as I go. That way I can watch it grow. I generally work off of a smaller area to make it larger right over the template itself. I create new motifs and small scrumbles, and attach them to the existing piece. I then work stitches into that larger piece in different directions until I feel the need to make another scrumble. I then start a new scrumble measuring it to the shape I need to fit into the template and sew that piece to the larger, assembled scrumble with the least amount of stitches possible to mimic the lace. If you choose to do it this way, very little finishing is required since you sew as you go. Some pieces of clothing require that two sides are made separately and then joined. Rather than seaming straight down the sides and over the shoulders or down the sleeves, line up the two pieces with about an inch between the two sections and fill in with lacy, mesh, or chain stitches, working back and forth from one piece to the other to make the join less obvious. I like to place a magazine or book under the area

of the garment I want to sew together to separate it from the rest of the garment and keep it flat.

Once the entire piece is joined, you can decide if you want to edge the whole piece with a single crochet or crab stitch to create a more finished look. I often leave the edge as it happens naturally in an irregular fashion.

Corners are funny things. When you want to create a corner or fill in to the corner of your template, you can use the old granny square method of 2 or 3 double crochets into the same stitch followed by 2 or 3 chains and then 2 or 3 double crochets into the same stitch. This gives you a nice squared-off edge if you need to take a turn to fit into the template. I try to follow the template as much as I can, but crochet is very forgiving, and you'll find fill-in stitches work very well to finish off edges after you've joined your scrumbles. Sometimes you end up with a larger hole in the lace than you wanted after all the scrumbles are assembled. Join a piece of yarn on one edge of the hole and chain to the other side. Single crochet to connect and you're done! You can add two or three lines of chains from one side to the other or just stitch right into the hole if it's particularly large. I like to try the clothes on as I make them. Sometimes an open area looks fine until you try it on and realize that the hole is in a place that might be revealing more than you'd like.

Yes, you can adjust the pieces to fit a template by using a steam iron to block but I seldom use blocking when I do organic scrumbling and usually only at the end after the garment is completed to give it a finishing touch. The truth is, with a scrumbled piece, if it's not hanging right when you make it, it probably never will. I'm more likely to take out whole areas of stitching and rework them rather than try to block it into place. If you do decide to block, use it sparingly. The decision to block has more to do with the yarn you are using. If you use a lace weight yarn, you may decide to lightly steam or spritz your pieces with water as you go and let them dry before joining the next pieces so they'll lay flat. Don't over block your piece or the fabric will end up being too limp.

My favorite method of ensuring a perfect fit when doing organic scrumbling is to use a dress form along with the template, or even in place of the template entirely. Dress forms are available at most fabric stores but you can also make one yourself using several different methods posted online; just do a Google search. I love the dress form I bought at my local fabric shop and use it for almost everything I make that's fitted. It's well worth the investment, and you'll end up using it more than you thought you would. At some point, when there are enough scrumbles or pieces done, pin together a few at strategic points, like the shoulders, and lay them on the dress form. You can then continue to make scrumbles and pin them right in place on the form rather than to the template. It gets a little tricky, but I like to crochet right on the piece as it is on the form to get a really fitted look. I continue to crochet new scrumbles and add them with fill-in stitches as I go, pinning the pieces to the dress form itself and crocheting in between. My dress form is sized to just slightly large than I am, so I know everything I make on it fits me perfectly when it's finished. I can see how something will hang and decide if I want to leave a hem asymmetrical or even it out. A dress form is a wonderful thing!

Beauty In Bloom

Organic Lace Scrumble Duster

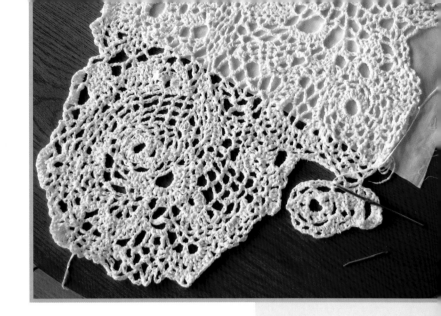

When I thought about this coat I knew I wanted to make it full length and I wanted to use some yummy silk chenille I'd been saving for a special project. Because of the size of the finished coat it was important it keep it lightweight so I used an I hook and more open stitches than I normally would for a smaller project. I started by tracing the outline of the back and one front side of a long sweater onto muslin fabric. I made scrumbles using the organic scrumble technique and joined them as I went, making more and filling in the template as needed.

Most of the scrumbles were as much as six to eight inches wide and very open to ensure the lacy look. I kept my eye on the overall piece as I made new scrumbles to make sure they fit into the template and blended well from one to the next. I filled in with stitches right up to the edges on all sides.

It was very handy to work on a table so I could move around the whole piece as I needed to and flip over sections to crochet back when necessary. As I made the larger scrumble pieces to add in, I worked on a separate piece of cardboard to ensure their flatness before

49

Sweet Romance

Organic Scrumble Cap-sleeved Blouse

I used a template made from an existing top initially but quickly moved the scrumbled pieces to a dress form once enough of them were made to hang properly from the shoulders. The rest of the scrumbles and fill-in stitches were done with the main area pinned to the form to get a closely shaped fit. Crocheting directly into a piece on a dress form is tricky but it can be done! It was important in this case to ensure the fit and see how the fabric would hang.

Once the piece was completed I used a single crochet around the edges and made crocheted button and loop closures.

Template modified from existing blouse

September Blush

Organic Scrumbled Tunic top with Filet Yoke

This adorable little tunic is made from a sport weight cotton yarn using a G hook. I started it from the top by creating a one piece filet yoke joined at the shoulders. I made the foundation chain the total bust size and worked up for a few rows and then created the front and backs from two balls of yarn, shaping with decreases to match my template as I continued up to the neckline and shoulders. The rest of the outfit was done over a template with the organic scrumbling technique, leaving an irregular organic feel to the edge. I joined the scrumbles to the main yoke by sewing them at strategic points.

The yarn was white originally and then hand-dyed after the piece was completed to create the variegated look.

The tunic template was created by tracing around an A-line dress and modifying it to be crocheted in pieces; yoke first as one piece and front and back separately.

Elegant Whisper

Organic Scrumble and Wild Irish Formal Lace Top

This luscious lace top was made with an H hook and a soft cotton worsted weight yarn. I made a template from an existing top and created a number of motifs to fit into the template. I then joined the motifs using a Wild Irish crochet fill-in stitch along with scrumbling a number of other crochet stitches to the edges.

Once the top was complete, it was embellished with a number of crocheted circles, flowers and dragonflies around the entire front neckline.

side view

Fortunate Touch
Celtic Lace Cuff

Inspired by a class I took at a CGOA national conference from Joan Davis, a wonderful crochet designer and teacher from Florida, I created this cuff bracelet using her Celtic Lace technique. She developed this style of crochet lace by combining traditional stitch techniques from Brugges lace and Celtic knot designs. The yarn is a fantastic, stretchy wool in a DK weight and I used an E hook.

After creating the cuff, I made several smaller strips of Celtic Lace and wound them through each other in a sculptural fashion. I added a few bead crocheted flowers and crocheted circles as embellishments along with a crocheted ball and loop closure.

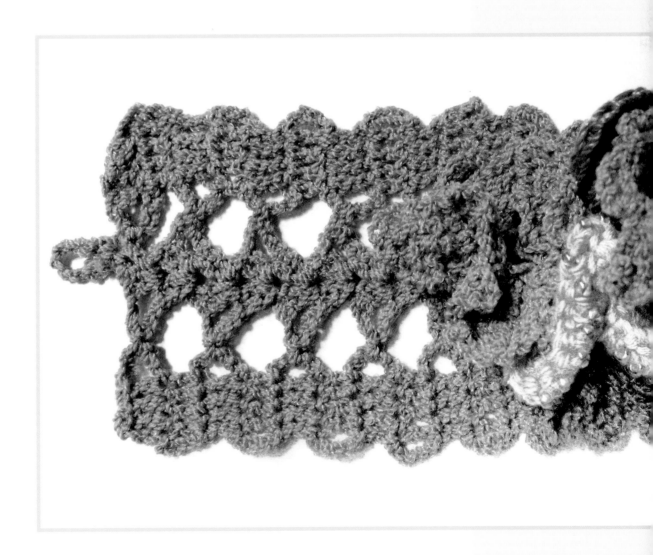

Geranium Slumber

Organic Scrumble Lace Pillow

This cozy pillow top was made for an existing, plain sofa pillow by cutting a piece of cardboard to the exact size of the finished square.

I used a wonderful hand-dyed merino and silk blend yarn and a G hook, starting with several large motifs. Each motif was joined to the next by various stitches, filling in to the edge of the square.

I repeated a simple shell pattern with a few single crochets in between around the entire outer edge to finish it off and give it a perfect square shape. The completed piece of fabric was then sewn to the pillow top with a blind hem stitch from the back. As you can see, it's quite comfy.

Summer Breeze

Wild Irish Crochet
and Brugges Lace Scarf

I created a number of random motifs using an H hook and white crochet cotton yarn and fit them closely together into a triangular shaped template for the body of this scarf.

Most of the single motifs were sewn together with fill-in stitches added as needed to fin-ish to the shape of the template. Once the body of the piece was completed I made a traditional wide ribbon of Brugges lace as the headband and tie. I then single crocheted around the outside edge, adding picots every 4 stitches.

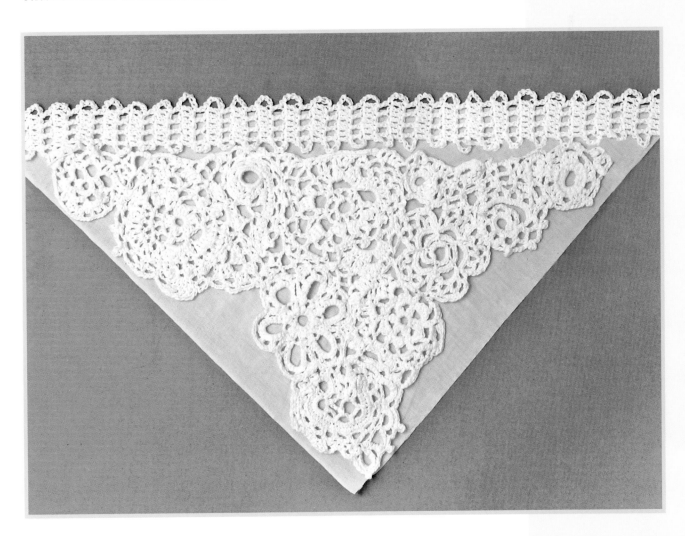

A scarf can be made from a simple triangle.

Lily of the Valley
Organic Scrumble Lace Shoulderbag

I used a high end cotton yarn in a DK weight to create this shoulder bag with a G hook. The yarn had a very earthy, natural quality to it so I wanted the final bag to reflect a casual, hippified appearance.

The body of the bag was made in one piece by creating a rectangular template for the front, back and flap. Once I filled in the entire form with scrumbles and joined them together, I filled in the spaces and edges to the outline. I then finished the edge with a single crochet.

To create the sides and a strap, I crocheted one long strip of rows of single crochet the length I wanted and sewed it into a continuous circle. I pinned the back and front to the edges of the long strap and sewed them on, allowing the flap to fold over the top.

Since the bag is a lace design, I chose to line it and found a perfect batik fabric to act as the background. I created a padded lining by sewing the batik to another piece of fabric and hand sewed it with a blind hem stitch to the inside of the bag and flap.

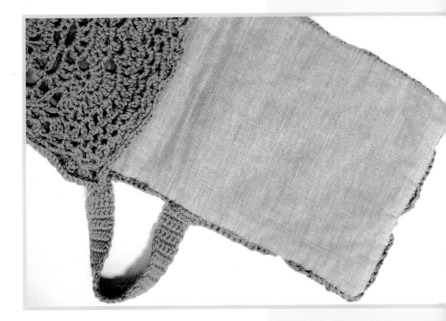

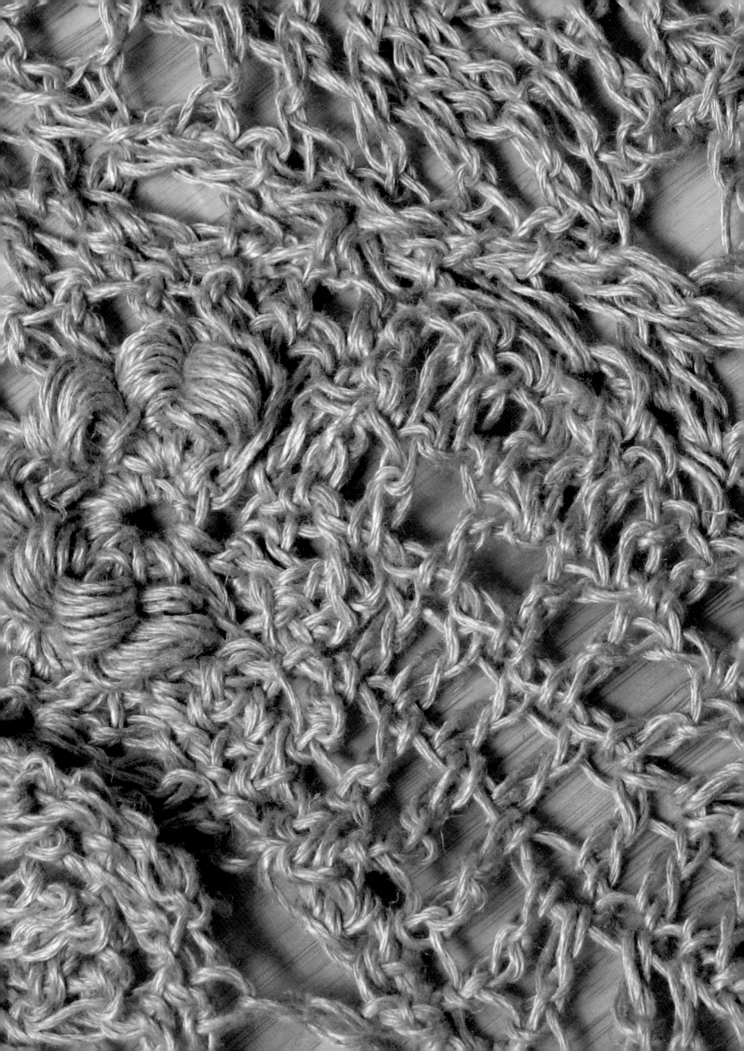

Gallery

Detail from cape by Dawn Jeffory-Nelson from page 92

Margaret Hubert

New York, USA

www.margarethubertoriginals.com

Margaret has had a long and interesting career in the needle arts since her start in 1963. In addition to running her own shop for 12 years, she spent many years as the needlework instructor for Bloomingdales in White Plains, New York.

Margaret has written numerous books on traditional and freeform crochet and knitting - some long out of print and others very recent. Most of those in print are available through her web site along with instructional DVDs and videos.

Margaret teaches freeform and other techniques nationally.

Prudence Mapstone
Brisbane, Australia

www.knotjustknitting.com

Prudence is a textile artist who has knitted for as long as she can remember, and taught herself to crochet back in her teens. Never one to follow the rules, she began designing her own intarsia knitwear in the '80s, and started working in a freeform manner more than 15 years ago.

Even though she loves to create highly textural and 'woolly' art-to-wear pieces, she also makes light and lacy garments more suitable for the sub-tropical climate where she lives.

Her work is constantly evolving, and she loves to incorporate different stitches and techniques into each new design. Color and texture are often the starting points for her creations. Prudence has sometimes been known to use more than 100 different yarns in the one piece, but for these two garments she has chosen a much more restrained approach, relying on the stitch patterns to create visual interest.

Prudence's work has been exhibited and on runways in many different countries. She enjoys sharing her techniques, and loves to encourage other crocheters and knitters to venture beyond the printed pattern.

Bonnie Pierce

Washington, USA

www.elegantcrochet.com

Bonnie is an internationally renowned freeform fiber artist, designer, author, exhibitor and bullion/roll stitch specialist. Her current works include items in five "On a Roll" books, Crochet! Magazine, Annie's scrap crochet series, Leisure Arts, American School of Needlework and several other hard back books. Bonnie has exhibited her freeform crochet and won awards in Israel, Australia, Wales, Chicago, Lacis Lace Museum in CA, Craft Adventure and Big E in Massachusetts.

She has taught classes at the Seattle Knitting and Fiber Arts Expo, Lacis lace museum in Berkeley CA and at Yarn Garden in Portland Oregon. Bonnie has exhibited freeform garments in Lacis museum's international display of freeform crochet. Her freeform garments were modeled in the Crochet Guild of America's Chain Link fashion show in Oakland in July 2005 and September 2007.
That year she was also named Interweave Press Piecework magazine's Crocheter of the Year.

Bonnie has had her work displayed at the Lacis Museum of Lace in Berkeley, CA and at the Museum of Arts and Design in NYC for the "Non-Conformist Crochet" demonstration.

Jennifer Hanson

California, USA

www.stitchdiva.com

Jennifer Hansen , founder and lead designer for Stitch Diva Studios, is known for her cutting edge vision. She is solely responsible for bringing hairpin lace into the modern age with her creative use of this traditional technique.

Jennifer lives in Fremont, California where she is a full-time crochet and knit designer, teacher and writer. Her innovative crochet work has been featured in various books, magazines and television shows including Vogue Knitting, Interweave Crochet, The Happy Hooker, The Encyclopedia of Crochet and Knitty Gritty.

She has been described as "One of the names that immediately comes to mind when thinking of the creative forces that have helped transport crochet from the realm of acrylic afghans to the sexy world of figure-flattering fashions." (Yarn Market News) Her professional background is in Architecture and Information Technology.

Hairpin lace is another great crochet lace technique to add to the mix for Freeform Crochet Lace. More info and a complete tutorial are available on the Stitch Diva website along with hairpin lace looms.

Close-up of hairpin lace from the skirt pictured on the opposite page.

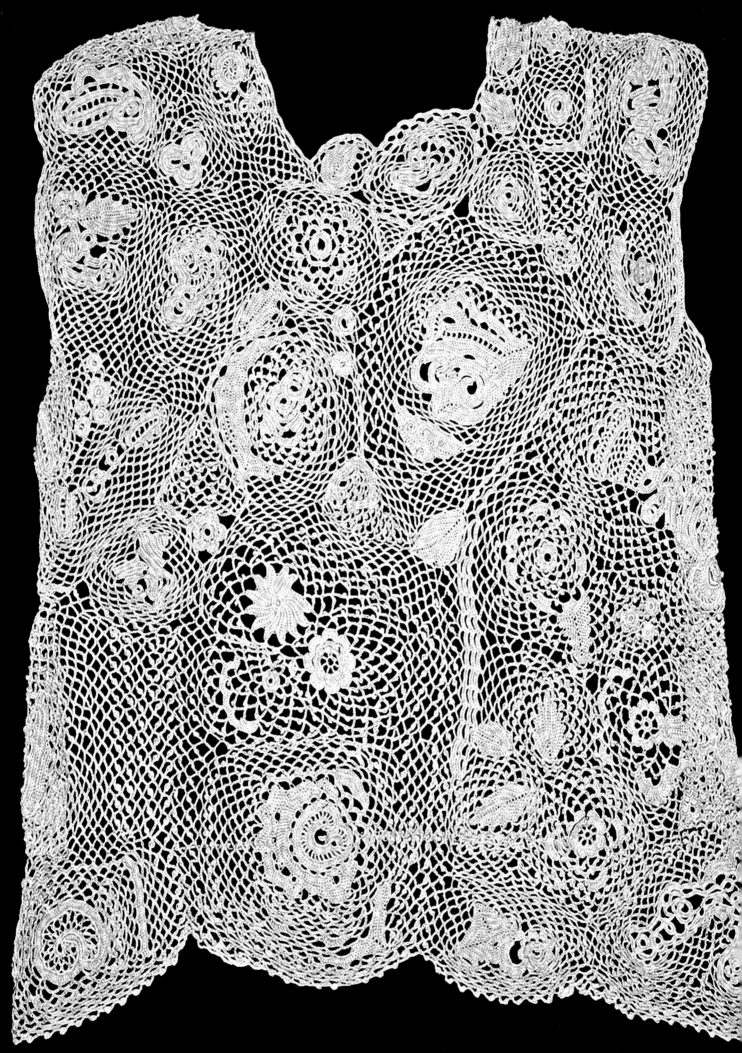

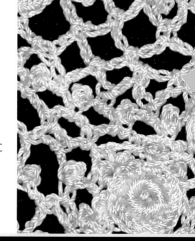

Pirkko Vega
Toronto, Canada

www.pirkkovega.net

Pirkko has been crocheting since she was very young, learning to crochet in public school in Finland.

Her sisters made lace edgings which she always admired for the delicacy of their work. It was not until years later with a move to Canada that she started to experiment with similar lace work and fell in love with Irish crochet because the designs were complicated but easy enough to do to produce amazing results.

Pirkko teaches crochet at a local yarn store along with exhibiting Irish Crochet and freeform crochet at annual exhibitions for local knitting groups and the International Freeform Crochet Guild.

Her pattern for a lovely crocheted bead necklace can be found in New Ideas for Today's Knitting by Jean Leinhauser.

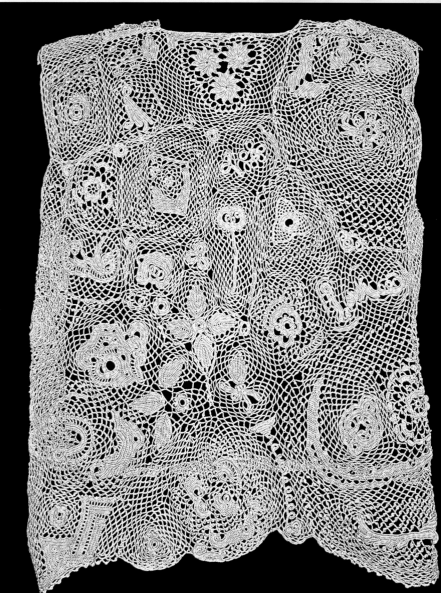

back view

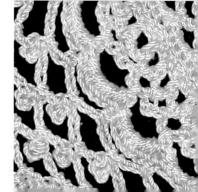

Resources and Bibliography

Freeform Books

Bullions and Beyond by Prudence Mapstone
Freeform: Serendipitous Design Techniques for Knitting & Crochet by Prudence Mapstone
      Available at www.knotjustknitting.com
Freeform Knitting and Crochet by Jenny Dowde
Freeformations by Jenny Dowde
Fun with Freeform Crochet by Margaret Hubert
How to Freeform Crochet by Margaret Hubert

Stitch and Motif Guides

24 Blocks on a Roll by Bonnie Pierce
99 Granny Squares to Crochet by Leisure Arts
101 Crochet Squares by Jean Leinhauser
200 Crochet Blocks for Blankets, Throws and Afghans by Jan Eaton
280 Crochet Shell Patterns by Darla Sims
Crochet Stitch Bible by Betty Barnden
Donna Kooler's Encyclopedia of Crochet by Donna Kooler
The Harmony Guides to Crochet Stitches (volumes 6 & 7) by Collins and Brown
The Complete Book of Crochet Stitch Designs: 500 Classic and Original Patterns by Linda Schapper

Crochet Lace Books

Amazing Crochet Lace by Doris Chan
Crochet Lace by Jean Leinhauser and Rita Weiss
Crocheted Lace by Pauline Turner
Clones Lace by Maire Treanor
Crochet Lace by Ondorisha
Favorite Irish Crochet Designs by Rita Weiss
Irish Crochet: Technique and Projects by Priscilla Publishing (Dover Needlework Series)

Out of Print Books:

Batsford Book of Crochet
The Crochet Workbook by Sylvia Cosh and James Walters
Favorite Filet Crochet Designs by Rita Weiss

Websites

Lacis is the best resource for books and publications on crochet lace along with tons of great hooks, yarns and threads perfect for crochet lace. They also have a lace museum and tons of examples of Irish crochet:
http://www.lacis.com

Interesting approaches and instructions from Hartmut Hass:
http://www.hassdesign.com

Incredible Hairpin Lace patterns and more!:
Stitch Diva Studios: Modern Crochet and Knit Designs:
http://www.stitchdiva.com/

James Walters and Sylvia Cosh:
http://www.crochet.nu/

The International Freeform Crochet Guild:
http://www.freeformcrochet.com/

Some of My Favorite Yarns

Tahki Cotton Classic Yarn, 100% mercerized cotton DK weight
Amore Colore Yarns, Gorgeous hand dyed yarns available at Stitch Cafe: http://www.stitchcafe.com
Patons Grace, 100% mercerized cotton DK weight
Habu Textiles: Incredible yarns made from natural materials
Southwest Trading Company: Tons of cool fibers, http://www.soysilk.com/yarn.html
Berroco Yarn Cotton Twist, 70% mercerized cotton & 30% rayon. Sport Weight
Debbie Bliss Cotton Cashmere, 85% Cotton, 15% Cashmere yarn DK weight
DMC Crochet Cottons: Traditions, Baroque, Senso and Cebelia threads
Lion Brand Lion Cotton, All natural 100% cotton, 4-ply worsted-weight yarn
Mango Moon Yarns Recycled Sari Silk
Shangri-La Crafts Banana Fiber Silk Yarn

And Hooks

Asciano Fiberarts Tools; Gorgeous rosewood hooks by Deborah Doyle
Clover Soft Touch Crochet Hooks
Hamanaka double ended Gold crochet hook
Addi Color Coded Crochet Hooks

About the Author

Myra Wood is an internationally known, award winning fiber & bead artist and designer. She teaches a wide range of classes in beading, embroidery, crochet and knitting, specializing in all things freeform. She's appeared on numerous episodes of Knitty Gritty and Uncommon Threads for the DIY & HGTV networks along with publishing a number of jewelry and clothing patterns in a wide range of books and magazines.

Classically trained in fine arts at the Pennsylvania Academy of Fine Arts, she has enjoyed a long career in the field of graphic arts and design. She lives in Los Angeles with her husband and 2 dogs.

Myra has been crocheting, sewing and crafting since she was young and enjoys any opportunity to inspire others creatively. She is also the moderator for the International Freeform Crochet Guild with over 1500 members worldwide and coordinator for their annual shows. Galleries of her work can be seen at www.myrawood.com